BLASTING OFF

ROCKETS THEN AND NOW

BLASTING OFF
ROCKETS THEN AND NOW

Steve Otfinoski

BENCHMARK BOOKS

MARSHALL CAVENDISH
NEW YORK

Benchmark Books
Marshall Cavendish Corporation
99 White Plains Road
Tarrytown, New York 10591-9001

Library of Congress Cataloging-in-Publication Data
Otfinoski, Steven.
Blasting off : rockets then and now / Steve Otfinoski.
    p.   cm. — (Here we go!)
Includes bibliographical references and index.
Summary: A simple introduction to the development of rockets from
their use by the Chinese in the thirteenth century to some of the many
kinds that exist in the twentieth century.
ISBN 0-7614-0611-5 (lb)
1. Rocketry—History—Juvenile literature. [1. Rocketry. 2. Rockets
(Aeronautics)] I. Title II. Series: Otfinoski, Steven. Here we go!
TL782.5.086   1999   629.47′5—dc21   97-15444   CIP   AC

Photo research by Matthew J. Dudley

Cover photo: *Corbis-Bettmann*

The photographs in this book are used by permission and through the
courtesy of: *The Image Bank:* Pete Turner, 1; Nick Nicholson, 2; Joseph
Drivas, 6-7; Erik Simonsen, 13 (top and bottom); T. I. Baker, 18; Frank
Whitney, 20; Dan Esgro, 21 (bottom); Larry Dale Gordon, 32; Rob Atkins,
back cover. *Corbis-Bettmann:* 7 (right), 8, 9 (top and bottom), 10, 11
(right), 16, 17 (right). *UPI/Corbis-Bettmann:* 11 (left), 12, 14 (top and
bottom), 15 (left and right), 21 (top). *Photo Researchers, Inc.:* Nasa-Foto,
17 (left); Hank Morgan, 19; David Parker-ESA-CNES/Arianespace/Science
Photo Library, 22, 24 (left); Jeff Greenberg/dMRg, 23; European Space
Agency/Science Photo Library, 24 (right), 25; Julian Baum/Science Photo
Library, 26; Nasa/Science Source, 27; George Baird/U.S. Army/Science
Photo Library, 28 (left), Ton Kinsbergen/Science Photo Library, 28-29;
Bruce Roberts, 30.

Printed in Hong Kong

6 5 4 3 2 1

To Matt,

for all the pictures that are out of this world

"...3...2...1...Blast Off!"
There is no more exciting moment than when a rocket leaves the launch pad and soars up, up, up into space. Modern rockets are little more than a half-century old, but people have dreamed about conquering space for centuries. The Chinese emperor above thought he could travel through the air in his "flying chair" powered by forty-seven small rockets. We don't know how far he got!

The Chinese probably invented rockets in the 1200s and used them as weapons of war. They were more like flying fireworks, but they gave the enemy a good scare. Nearly six hundred years later the British developed a sixty-pound rocket that carried explosives. They used them to bombard Fort William McHenry during the War of 1812. Francis Scott Key watched the battle and wrote of "the rockets' red glare" in our national anthem, "The Star-Spangled Banner."

A few years later people dreamed of larger rockets that could travel into space. These two cartoons show rockets carrying people as far as the moon. At the time, most people thought space travel was a joke.

This "human rocket" took to the sky in 1882, but quickly returned to Earth with its parachute. Other rocket builders were more scientific and practical.

THE PARACHUTES

In 1926, Robert Goddard, an American scientist, launched a ten-foot-long rocket fueled by gasoline and liquid oxygen. It rose 421 feet into the air. "It looked almost magical as it rose," Goddard later wrote in his diary. The space age had begun.

The U.S. military later became interested in Goddard's work with rockets. In World War II the Germans developed a rocket missile called the V-2. After the war, many German scientists came to the United States and continued their work with rockets.

Today, rocket weapons like the Navy's Tomahawk cruise missile (above) can fly many miles before zeroing in on an enemy target. Some scientists have proposed a Strategic Defense Initiative (SDI). It calls for a satellite (below) that could intercept enemy missiles in space before they strike the United States.

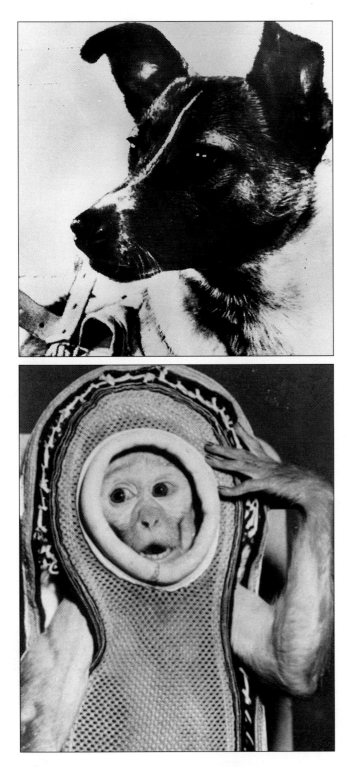

In the 1950s, scientists used rockets to explore outer space. In October 1957, the Soviets launched *Sputnik I,* the first artificial satellite to orbit the earth. *Sputnik II* was sent up a month later with a passenger—a husky dog named Laika.

Early U.S. satellites carried monkeys onboard. Miss Sam looks uneasy about her space suit. Her eight-minute flight was a success, though, and she returned safely to Earth.

In May 1961, the United States sent its first human astronaut into space. Alan Shepard takes a last look out of his space capsule before take-off in a Redstone-Mercury rocket. His fifteen-minute flight was the first of many manned U.S. space flights.

Nine years after Shepard's flight, astronauts Neil Armstrong and "Buzz" Aldrin went to the moon aboard the *Apollo 11* (opposite). They landed on the moon in their lunar capsule the *Eagle* (above left), which looked more like a giant spider than a bird. Armstrong was the first earthling to walk on the moon's surface (above right). He called it "one small step for a man, one giant leap for mankind." Millions of awestruck people back on Earth watched the event on live television.

In the early days, sections of a rocket would drop off at different stages and burn up in the earth's atmosphere. Finally just the capsule carrying the astronauts was left to hurtle through space. Then scientists developed a new rocket, the space shuttle, that could be used over and over again. Above, the space shuttle *Columbia* is being carried to its launching pad on a machine called a crawler. Then comes the countdown, and the rocket blasts off. Can you see the two rocket boosters on the sides and the large external tank that holds the fuel?

Two minutes after blast-off, the booster rockets separate from the main rocket and parachute to Earth. The external tank is released and drops to Earth just before the rocket goes into orbit. As part of their mission, the astronauts aboard this shuttle link up with a satellite already in space.

They leave the rocket and repair the satellite.
When their mission is completed, the shuttle returns to
Earth and lands smoothly on a runway, just like an airplane.

What makes a rocket roar into space? Fuel, also called propellant, ignites inside the rocket and creates hot gases that rush out of the rear nozzles (above). This thrust causes the rocket to move in the opposite direction. Rocket engines (left) must be big and powerful to create enough thrust for the rocket to escape the pull of gravity.

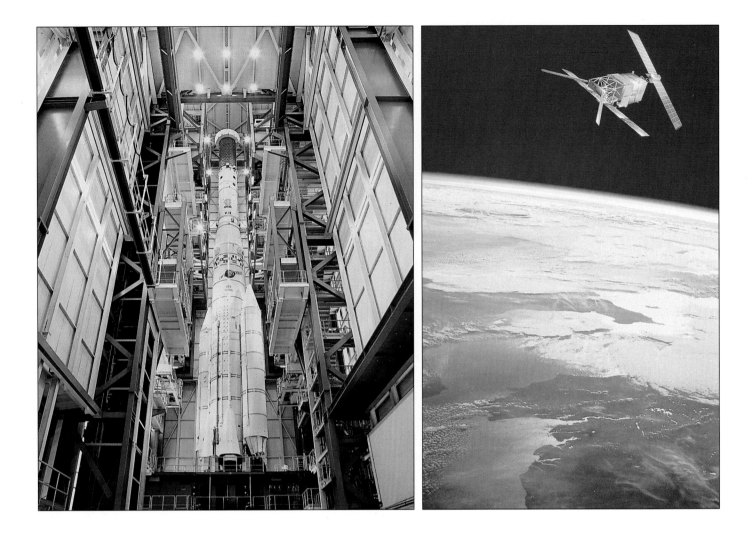

This Ariane 4 rocket being prepared for launching will carry three satellites into space. The weather satellite on the right was launched from a rocket. It records and studies ice formations on the earth below. The information it collects will help scientists better understand how climate changes occur.

A communications satellite is being launched with this rocket. These satellites relay television, radio, or telephone signals between one place on Earth and another.

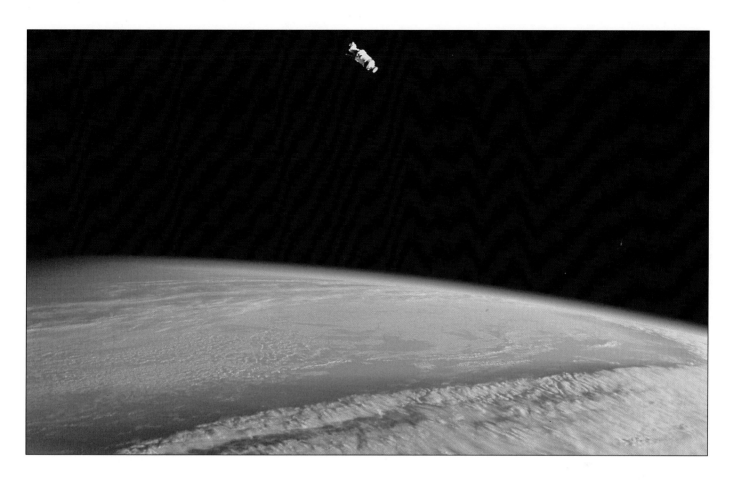

Still other rocket-launched satellites, called space probes, travel to distant planets to gather new information about them. The *Voyager 2* (illustration, left) is taking pictures of one of Neptune's moons and relaying them back to Earth. The satellite above is called the *Ulysses.* It is exploring the planet Jupiter and will then pay a visit to the Sun to learn more about its fiery surface. Like the Greek hero it is named after, the *Ulysses* travels far from home!

Delta Clipper (DC-X), 1993

Rockets have taken humans to the Moon and back. They have carried satellites into every corner of our solar system. Someday everyone may be an astronaut, traveling in fast-moving rockets to explore new worlds beyond our solar system. What will we find, out there in the darkness of deep space?

Solar and Heliospheric Observatory (SOHO), illustration, 1995

INDEX

Armstrong, Neil 17
Goddard, Robert 11
launch pad 7, 18
lift-off 23
missiles 12, 13

rocket boosters 18, 20
rocket launched satellites
     14, 24, 25, 27
Shepard, Alan 15
space capsule 15, 18

space shuttle 18, 20
Sputnik I 14
Tomahawk missile 13

FIND OUT MORE

Asimov, Isaac. *Piloted Space Flights.* Milwaukee, Wisc.: Gareth Stevens Publishing, 1990.

————. *Rockets, Probes, and Satellites.* Milwaukee, Wisc.: Gareth Stevens Publishing, 1988.

Branley, Franklyn M. *The Story of the Space Shuttle: Columbia and Beyond.* New York: William Collins Publishers, 1979.

Burch, Jonathan. *Astronauts.* Ada, Okla.: Garrett Educational Corporation, 1992.

English, June, and James, Thomas D. *Mission: Earth Voyage to the Home Planet.* New York: Scholastic, 1996.

STEVE OTFINOSKI has written more than sixty books for children. He also has a theater company called *History Alive!* that performs plays for schools about people and events from the past. Steve lives in Stratford, Connecticut, with his wife and two children.